Understanding Diseases and Disorders

Alzheimer's Disease

Barbara Webber

KIDHAVEN PRESS

An imprint of Thomson Gale, a part of The Thomson Corporation

Detroit • New York • San Francisco • San Diego • New Haven, Conn. • Waterville, Maine • London • Munich

THOMSON
™
GALE

Cover photo: PhotoDisc
CC Studio/Photo Researchers, Inc., 21
John Cole/Photo Researchers, Inc., 25
© Owen Franken/CORBIS, 32
© Rick Friedman/CORBIS, 8
© Michal Heron/CORBIS, 15
© Ronnie Kaufman/CORBIS, 11
© Stephanie Maze/CORBIS, 27
© Tom & Dee Ann McCarthy/CORBIS, 31

Will & Deni McIntyre/Photo Researchers, Inc., 5
Mendil/Photo Researchers, Inc., 18
© Gabe Palmer/CORBIS, 39
PhotoDisc, 35, 37, 39 (inset)
© Pete Saloutos/CORBIS, 34
John Sher/Photo Researchers, Inc., 17
Siu/Photo Researchers, Inc., 22
Steve Zmina, 7, 13, 28

This book is dedicated to Ethel Webber, the best mother one could have. In spite of Alzheimer's, sweet to the end.

LIBRARY OF CONGRESS CATALOGING-IN-PUBLICATION DATA

Webber, Barbara, 1946-
  Alzheimer's disease / by Barbara Webber.
    p. cm. — (Understanding diseases and disorders)
  Summary: Defines Alzheimer's disease and discusses how it is
  diagnosed and treated.
  Includes bibliographical references.
  ISBN 0-7377-2165-0
  1. Alzheimer's disease—Juvenile literature. I. Title. II. Series.
  RC523.W425 2005
  616.8'31—dc22   2004002670

Printed in the United States of America

Contents

Chapter One

What Is Alzheimer's Disease?

Memory is the base of all human thought, understanding, and action. The brain is the center for all memories. It is made of nerve tissue and has many sections connected by nerve cells. The sections make sense of sights, sounds, tastes, touches, and feelings. They are known as the **cerebral hemispheres**. Deep inside the hemispheres is the **hippocampus**, which transfers information into memory.

When the brain and its memory connections are working properly, tasks such as eating, sleeping, talking, and thinking are done with ease. A well-functioning brain instantly remembers how to swallow, nap, speak, and understand. Healthy brains allow new ideas to be added to our knowledge bank every day.

If brain tissue is damaged or destroyed, the ability to reason, remember, and learn is harmed. This is called **dementia**. Brain cells can be hurt in many ways. Some causes of destroyed brain cells are head wounds, strokes, and **infections**. Alzheimer's disease (AD) is a disease that destroys brain cells. It is the most common form of more than sixty types of dementia. No one has yet found out what causes dying brain tissue in people

Alzheimer's disease affects this man's short-term memory, and he has trouble remembering his wife's name.

with AD. Because scientists do not know what causes AD, they do not know how to keep people from getting it or how to cure it.

The Alzheimer's Puzzle

Alzheimer's slowly takes away a person's memories. First, short-term recall disappears. AD sufferers cannot remember people's names. They forget how to do things such as brushing their teeth and writing checks. Later, they lose their long-term memories. Important pictures vanish from their minds. They cannot remember where they grew up or even what their parents looked like.

Alzheimer's changes people. As it advances, it affects their ability to talk, eat, and sleep normally. It can alter a person's personality, too. A person with AD can lose his or her sense of humor and kindness and become angry and even violent.

Today more than 4 million people live with Alzheimer's disease in the United States. AD is an old people's disease. Most people who get it are over sixty-five. Fifty percent of people over the age of eighty-five have it. It is not **contagious**, so it cannot be passed from one person to another, like a cold. It affects more women than men.

Alzheimer's is **progressive** and permanent. This means it goes through stages that worsen and always lead to death. Once a person learns from a doctor that he or she has Alzheimer's disease, he or she usually lives eight to ten years longer.

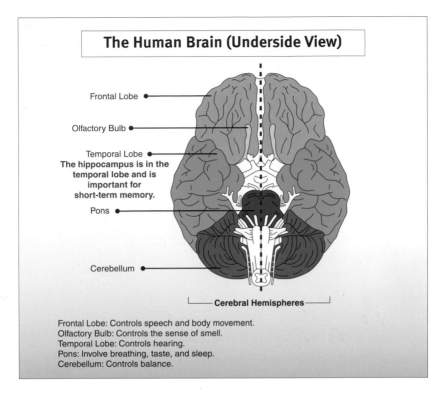

The Human Brain (Underside View)

Frontal Lobe

Olfactory Bulb

Temporal Lobe
The hippocampus is in the temporal lobe and is important for short-term memory.

Pons

Cerebellum

Cerebral Hemispheres

Frontal Lobe: Controls speech and body movement.
Olfactory Bulb: Controls the sense of smell.
Temporal Lobe: Controls hearing.
Pons: Involve breathing, taste, and sleep.
Cerebellum: Controls balance.

During that time the person slowly loses more and more skills. He or she also shows more noticeable changes in behavior.

An Alarming Discovery

Alzheimer's disease was first diagnosed more than one hundred years ago. In 1901 Dr. Alois Alzheimer was working in a mental hospital in Frankfurt, Germany. There, he met a woman named Auguste D., who showed many signs of dementia. She often exploded with anger for no apparent reason. She accused her husband of doing things he had not done. She used strange words for simple objects, like *milk jug* for *cup*.

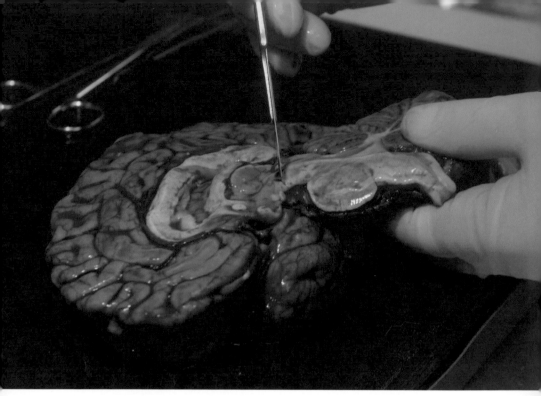

A researcher examines human brain tissue for signs of Alzheimer's disease.

Alzheimer saw her become more and more confused until she died five years later. After her death, he looked at her brain under a microscope. It was shrunken and dry. He found two surprises in the outermost layer of the cerebral hemispheres of her brain. First, he discovered a bundle of dead nerve cells, which were later named **tangles**. Next, he noticed round, sticky globs, today known as **plaques**. No one had ever been aware of these odd clusters before.

This discovery led doctors and scientists to later discoveries. They learned that people who had tangles, plaques, and irregular brains had a particular kind of dementia. Today, this kind of dementia is called Alzheimer's after the doctor who first identified it. Scientists also found that this type of dementia was seen most in older people. It could, however, affect younger adults. Auguste D. started to show signs of it when she was fifty-one. This was at least fifteen years earlier than most AD cases.

A Family Connection

When AD is found in adults in their thirties, forties, or fifties, it is called early-onset Alzheimer's. This type is **genetic**, or inherited from a family member. For example, Hannah, who lived in Latvia during the 1800s, got AD when she was about forty-six years old. Four of her nine children and eleven of her thirty-four grandchildren also got it. Compared with AD in the elderly, early-onset AD is uncommon.

No matter what age one is when Alzheimer's strikes, it develops gradually. All people who get the disease will pass through several levels of worsening **symptoms**.

How AD Develops

Alzheimer's advances in three major stages. In the first stage, the AD victim knows something is wrong, but no one else does. During the second stage, everyone knows there is a memory problem. By the time the third stage appears, caregivers, friends, and family know the victim has Alzheimer's. The victim, however, has such severe brain damage that he or she is no longer aware of his or her condition.

The beginning stage is called the early or mild stage. At this point, people with AD start to repeat themselves often. Family and friends find this very annoying, but the AD sufferer cannot help it. Faulty brain cell connections are to blame. Charlie, a middle-school student from Takoma Park, Maryland, remembers when his grandmother first showed signs of having Alzheimer's. He says, "One very hot summer day she told me to put on a sweater. I told her many times I was not cold, but she kept repeating herself every few minutes. Finally, my mother came with ice cream. She changed my grandmother's attention from sweaters to eating."[1]

Other behaviors also appear in stage one. Putting objects in unusual places (like underwear in the oven or a checkbook in a box of cookies) is common. The AD sufferer forgets events that have just happened. Forgetting people's names and the words for places and things also occurs often. When the person with AD tries to remember a particular word and it will not come to mind, it is very frustrating. This behavior can be upsetting to the person with AD because it is a constant reminder to him or her that something is wrong.

Alzheimer's typically affects the elderly, but a form of the disease can be passed down to younger generations.

Middle-stage Alzheimer's, also called the moderate stage, is the time when AD is usually **diagnosed** by doctors. This can be an unsafe time for Alzheimer victims. During this period, AD sufferers might forget to turn off appliances, such as stoves and irons. They also forget to eat meals and may no longer be able to read.

Another problem that may occur regularly at this stage is wandering. Amy, an activity director at an adult day care center in Virginia, describes a time when this happened:

> One day, although all doors were locked, a man named Robert found a garden gate open. He walked away from the Center. When staff members realized he was gone, we searched the area. We could not find Robert anywhere. When his wife came to pick him up, he was still missing. Later, I got a call from a nursing home more than two miles away, across a busy highway. The caller was the nursing home director. He said someone had seen a man walking around, looking lost. Since he was wearing a **Safe Return** bracelet, he was brought to the nursing home. We sent his wife to the home and Robert was soon safely back with his family. [2]

The last stage is severe AD. By this time, plaques and tangles have harmed so many areas of

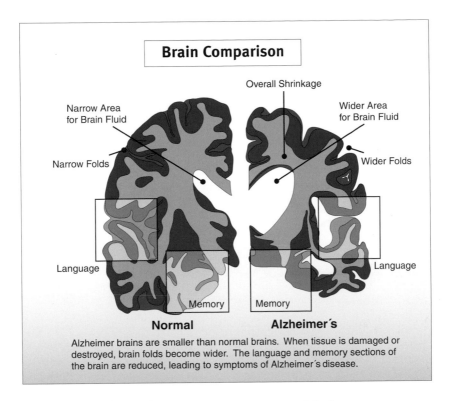

Brain Comparison

Overall Shrinkage

Narrow Area
for Brain Fluid

Wider Area
for Brain Fluid

Narrow Folds

Wider Folds

Language

Language

Memory

Memory

Normal

Alzheimer's

Alzheimer brains are smaller than normal brains. When tissue is damaged or destroyed, brain folds become wider. The language and memory sections of the brain are reduced, leading to symptoms of Alzheimer's disease.

the brain that the patient cannot think, reason, or talk. The person needs help with everything, even going to the bathroom. He or she has trouble chewing and swallowing. Finally, he or she is kept in bed. At the end, the patient dies. Death is not usually from AD itself but instead comes from problems brought on by Alzheimer's, such as heart disease, infections, or inability to eat.

People with AD and their caregivers hope that scientists will soon find a way to cure AD or at least prevent it. Until that day, the best that can be done is to discover Alzheimer's disease in a person as early as possible. This allows AD victims to get the best help available.

Chapter Two

Diagnosing the Disease

I t is important to recognize Alzheimer's disease as early as possible. This will help the patient and family have more time to find the best **treatments** and care.

The Rising Mystery

In its early stage, AD is difficult to identify. Normal elderly people do some of the same things as people showing the first signs of AD. They may take longer to remember things and sometimes forget where they put things. That is why it is hard, at first, to tell who has AD. Another problem is that some families ignore AD changes. Families are sometimes too busy to notice early changes. Also, people with the disease sometimes try to hide it. Some make jokes about their mistakes or pretend everything is fine.

There are clues that suggest a medical problem exists. One of the first to appear is constant repeating. Another is the use of wrong words to name simple objects. For example, a tree may be called a flower, or a pen may be called a writer. Additional signs are losing things and placing things where they do not belong. An example is putting wallets or purses in the refrigerator. People with Alzheimer's often do not know what year, day, or time it is.

Because this Alzheimer's patient has trouble doing basic tasks like dressing, she lives in the Alzheimer's unit of a nursing home.

Calendars and clocks do not help them because they no longer understand what the dates and times mean. They have trouble doing basic things such as dressing, cooking, or driving. Personality and mood changes sometimes appear. People that were once fun-loving and happy become angry or sad. When these actions happen regularly, some type of dementia exists.

Families are often confused when their loved ones show signs of AD. They do not know why such odd behavior is appearing. They do not know how to help them until they get a diagnosis. Lurli, a retired schoolteacher, was sad but relieved when she found out her mother had Alzheimer's. She finally had an explanation for her mother's problems. She says, "By having a name for the illness, I could get information about it. I could get proper medicines for my mother. I was able to find ways to deal with my mother's unusual behavior."[3] Early diagnosis led Lurli to the best treatments that could be found. When a person exhibits dementia-like behaviors regularly, he or she must be examined by a doctor to get an accurate diagnosis.

A Challenging Diagnosis

It is not easy for doctors to make a diagnosis when they first see patients with memory problems. The only way to be 100 percent positive that a patient has AD is to look at his or her brain tissue

A doctor reviews an elderly patient's medical history to determine if he is at risk for Alzheimer's.

under a microscope. Since this can only be done after a patient dies, the doctor must use other ways to identify the problem.

First, the doctor considers the behaviors that look like AD. Some signs of dementia are caused by something other than AD, such as strokes, a lack of vitamins, or brain injuries. These other sources must be ruled out.

Testing to determine the cause of memory loss takes time. The doctor first looks at the patient's health records to learn about his or her medical history. An exam of the patient's body follows.

A therapist tests an elderly woman for Alzheimer's by asking her to identify common objects.

The patient undergoes blood and urine tests, and brain X-rays, called CAT scans, are taken, too.

Finally, the patient answers questions. He or she also takes written tests. This helps the doctor learn how much damage has already been done to the brain. Memory and language are two areas measured. Patients might be shown pictures and then be asked to name the objects they see. Perhaps they will have to count backward, for example, from thirty-five to twenty-five. Sometimes they are told to draw shapes or copy patterns.

The clock test asks dementia victims to draw a clock and then put the correct numbers on its face. Next they are given a time and are asked to draw an hour hand and a minute hand pointing to that given time. Few people with dementia can do this test correctly. Doctors can give the same tests again at a later date so they can study the rate of a patient's memory loss.

This complete testing allows doctors to tell patients what disorder they have. Doctors may decide a patient has a different type of dementia or either possible or probable Alzheimer's. *Possible* means that the doctor thinks the patient has AD in combination with another illness. *Probable* means that all other conditions have been ruled out and it is most likely AD. Doctors are now able to make a correct diagnosis of Alzheimer's disease nine out of ten times.

Seeking a diagnosis early in the course of the disease is good for the patient and his or her family. It gives them the most possible time to plan for Alzheimer-related problems that will have to be dealt with as the disease progresses. Porter Shimer is the author of a book about Alzheimer's disease. He writes, "Being tested for AD can be the single most important step against this disease that families can encourage their loved ones to take."[4]

Getting a diagnosis of probable Alzheimer's is upsetting. Learning they have an incurable disease is difficult for victims. They might have feelings of fear, hopelessness, sadness, or anger. It is also troubling for the patient's family, who may wonder what to do. But there are sources available for help.

Locating Help

Doctors, nurses, and health care workers offer good advice to the AD patient and his or her family. They can explain about AD medicines that will help if they are taken right away. They can suggest drugs to help the patient sleep and offer special diets and procedures that will make it easier for patients to eat and swallow pills.

The group that offers the most help to families of AD victims is the Alzheimer's Association. This organization provides services for people learning to cope with AD. Many local chapters have training programs for families, group meetings for those in the early stages of the disease, and a telephone help line for any questions about Alzheimer's. The association can assist AD victims who live alone, and it also offers support groups. At these meetings, family caregivers can talk to each other and learn particular methods to handle AD. Alzheimer's Association staff members know what community resources are available and can therefore advise families about home care assistance, adult day care centers, and nursing homes. They know names of lawyers for the elderly and providers of transportation for patients who can no longer drive. In addition, local chapters give away AD information booklets. They also have libraries that loan current books, videos, and audiotapes that provide a wealth of information about the disease.

Lawyers who work with an AD victim and his or her family can provide several important

Brain scans allow doctors to find deformities in a patient's brain that might indicate Alzheimer's disease.

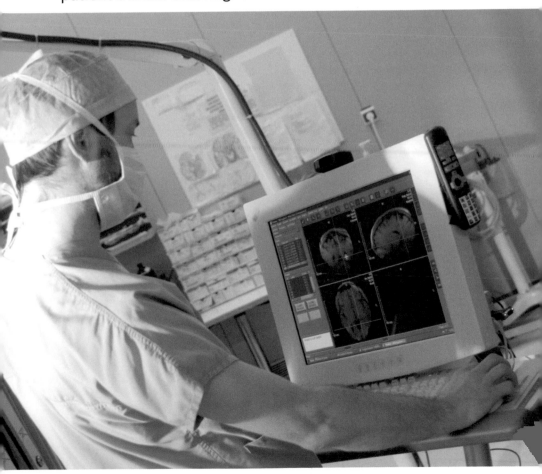

A researcher tests a man for Alzheimer's by timing
how long he takes to match geometric shapes to their
cutouts.

services. They can create a will for the patient if the disease is in an early stage. They can also name one family member or friend to make lawful choices for the AD patient. This becomes necessary if the patient needs medical care but cannot understand what is happening to him or her. It is especially important during AD's final stage, when the person with AD can no longer make his or her own decisions.

Taking care of a person with AD is not easy. Since there is no cure, caregivers cannot get rid of the disease. The best they can do is to accept help that is available and make life as pleasant as possible for the victim.

Chapter Three

Living with Alzheimer's

Many victims of Alzheimer's move in with family members after they get an AD diagnosis. Living with Alzheimer's is a challenge not only for the AD sufferer but also for those who care for him or her. The goal for those who care for AD victims is to make the patient's life as good as it can be, despite the disease. This can be done with thoughtful caregiving that treats AD sufferers in a special way. It requires time and patience, but it provides AD patients with an improved quality of life.

Caregiving at Home

The people who take care of AD victims are called caregivers. Most often they are family members.

Professional doctors and home care workers are caregivers, too.

Capable caregivers make sure the AD victim receives the best care. They must keep the patient safe and comfortable. They must help the person with AD keep his or her self-respect. This can be done by keeping the person clean and presentable, talking to him or her calmly without argument, and finding activities and simple tasks he or she

Alzheimer's patients at an advanced stage of the disease often need full-time care in a nursing home.

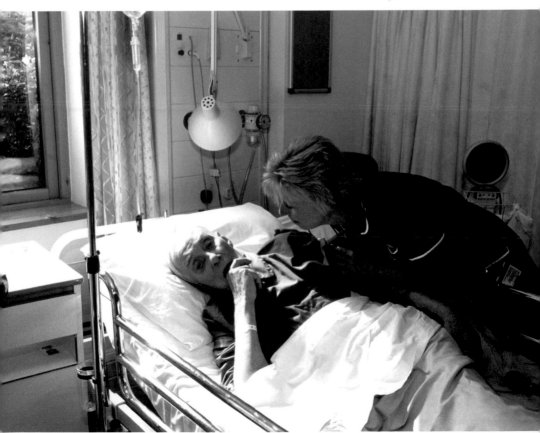

can enjoy. Sympathetic caregiving works as well as any AD drugs that are now available.

Caring for an AD patient is a challenging job. A good caregiver must keep the AD sufferer alert and active all day. This can be done by playing easy games with him or her or by sharing specially designed AD videos. The patient can be encouraged to do simple tasks, such as folding clothes or sharpening pencils. Having conversations about the past also helps, as does singing and listening to music with the patient. Caregivers can give the AD patient medicine that will help him or her sleep restfully every night. The caregiver must bathe, feed, and dress the patient and keep him or her from wandering away. Caregivers must do all these tasks knowing that the patient will get worse instead of better.

One person cannot do this alone because it becomes too stressful. The main caregiver needs help from many people. If children are part of the adult caregiver's family, they can be included. They can begin by learning about Alzheimer's. Books about AD can be found at their school or at local libraries. Their local Alzheimer's Association has pamphlets about AD. Parents can share the facts with children and tell them what they can do to help.

One thing children might do is share family photo albums. Asking questions about the past often helps, too. They could make and hang

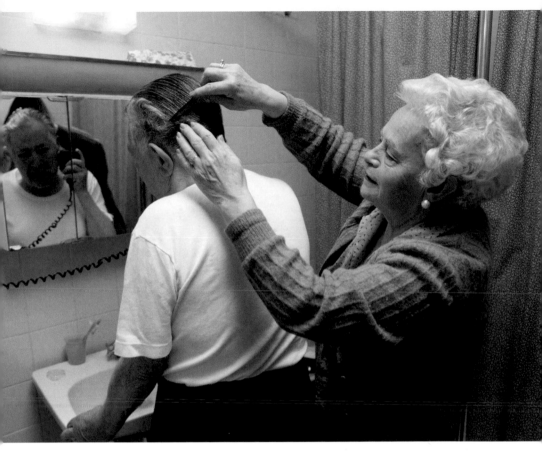

An Alzheimer's patient shaves with an electric razor as his wife combs his hair for him.

signs that name objects in the house (such as a sink or a closet). This will help the Alzheimer sufferers when they cannot remember words. Singing simple songs also helps. People with AD feel happy when they can remember words to songs, even easy ones such as "Old MacDonald Had a Farm."

As Alzheimer's progresses, the AD sufferer's appearance and actions become strange to those

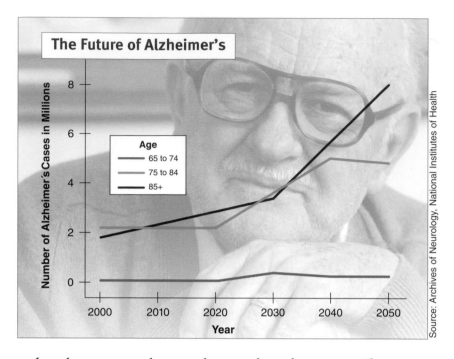

The Future of Alzheimer's

Number of Alzheimer's Cases in Millions

Age
— 65 to 74
— 75 to 84
— 85+

Year

Source: Archives of Neurology, National Institutes of Health

who know nothing about the disease. The AD patient might wear unmatched shoes or put on a coat in hot weather. At times he or she might stare blankly into space. His or her speech may not make sense. This can be embarrassing and upsetting, especially for children. An example is Eva from western Virginia. When Eva's grandmother got AD, she moved in with Eva, her husband, and her two daughters. "Eight-year-old Blair and ten-year-old C.J. used to have their friends visit all the time," Eva says. "They had lots of sleepovers here, too. Once grandmother moved in, that stopped. We did not know what she would do or say. We did not want the girls to feel uneasy. We did not know what else to do."[5] One way to deal with embarrassing situations is to explain the disease to friends and relatives. Once they understand why they will see odd behavior and know that the patient has an incurable disease, they are more accepting and sympathetic.

Current research shows that caregivers will be more successful dealing with AD victims if they use a method called validation therapy. With this system, caregivers do not argue with patients or try to convince them that they are wrong. They try to accept what patients have said (even if it is not correct) and then gently change the subject. For example, when AD sufferer Ethel said she wanted to take a walk to visit her sister (who lived several hundred miles away), her caregiver, Barbara, did not try to argue or explain why she could not. Instead, she suggested that Ethel's sister might not be home, but she and Ethel could take a walk to the park and see the roses.

Even with family help, caring for an AD sufferer can be an exhausting job. Home care services provide a way for the main caregiver to get a break from his or her difficult situation. Home care workers come to the patient's house. They help with all caregiving chores and make sure the person with AD does not wander away. Home care, though, is expensive. Another drawback is that it cannot provide the group activities that most AD sufferers enjoy.

Caregiving Away from Home

There are places that do offer group activities and many other benefits to those with Alzheimer's.

They are called adult day care centers. At these centers, the AD sufferer can spend time each day with many caregivers. The staff members at adult centers are trained to work with people in the earlier stages of AD. Adult centers also help the patient's main caregivers, who can leave their sick loved one in the hands of attentive people and not have to worry about him or her. This gives caregivers a chance to have some time for themselves.

At the centers, each planned activity happens at the same time every day. People with AD like this because it is familiar. The day care staff also encourages everyone to move and dance for exercise. Staff members frequently talk with AD patients about events that happened a long time ago. This helps keep those with Alzheimer's alert. Simple arts-and-crafts projects and short field trips are also included in the schedules of many day care centers.

Music is often used daily at adult centers. Sing-alongs are popular. AD victims remember words for songs long after they have forgotten many other words. Ben, the musical director for a center run by the Jefferson Area Board for the Aging, explains, "Music is very helpful. It is one of the last things to be lost. Many people with AD can play an instrument or sing when they cannot do so many other things anymore. It gives them many moments of happiness."[6]

Because they provide such full and active programs, adult day care centers are successful.

However, when AD sufferers reach the late stage of Alzheimer's, they must find round-the-clock caregivers. At this point, a nursing home with a special area for patients with AD becomes necessary.

Modern adult care centers and nursing homes are being designed and built with special features for AD patients. They might include vegetable and flower gardens, circular pathways (to prevent wandering away), and exercise equipment. They

Alzheimer's patients in adult day care centers are encouraged to participate in exercise activities such as dancing.

A physical therapist works with a group of Alzheimer's patients in an adult day care center.

may be built near preschools, so the elderly and the young can enjoy time together. Many health care workers are learning how to use validation therapy. These improvements also raise the quality of life for those with AD.

Chapter Four

Treatment and Prevention

In addition to thoughtful caregiving, the only other treatment available to victims of AD is a limited number of medications. Because of this, and the fact that a cure for the disease is not expected for years, **prevention** is the current best hope for a future without Alzheimer's.

Helpful Drugs

Since the 1990s, several drugs have been made just for Alzheimer's. They work by slowing the formation of plaques and tangles. They are helpful when taken during the early stages of AD. They do not make memory better, but for a while they keep memory loss from getting worse. They only work, however, for half the people who have AD.

A therapist helps an Alzheimer's sufferer to improve hand-eye coordination by bouncing a ball off a trampoline.

The latest AD drug, called memantine, is the first one made for the later stages of the disease. It lowers glutamate, a substance that scientists believe damages and kills brain cells. Some people who have taken it show a slight improvement in memory and in performing tasks of daily living. Others show a reduction of anger or agitation. Like other AD drugs, memantine does not stop the advance of the disease.

Other problems that AD sufferers have can be handled with commonly prescribed drugs. Examples are pills that bring on sleep or act against depression. Some fight hallucinations, visions that people see that are not real. Others act against delusions, ideas that people have that are not true, such as thinking someone is trying to steal their things.

The search for improved AD drugs and a cure continues, but the focus of most current AD **research** is on ways to keep Alzheimer's from starting.

Prevention

Once Alzheimer's disease starts, it does not stop. Therefore, a main goal of AD researchers is to create

Alzheimer's sufferers may take a wide variety of drugs to fight different symptoms of the disease.

a **vaccine** that will prevent Alzheimer's. In 1999, after many experiments on mice, scientists thought they had made the first AD vaccine. When they tried it on humans, however, it caused brain swelling in some people and was quickly withdrawn. This early attempt has led to more recent experiments for a better version of the vaccine. Researchers at Thomas Jefferson University in Pennsylvania are hopeful that a vaccine they have been using successfully on monkeys will work for people, too. It is possible that a safe vaccine to prevent Alzheimer's disease will be available by 2015.

Healthy Living

Until a vaccine is developed, people must try to prevent AD in other ways. Present-day research suggests that having a healthy lifestyle can help people avoid many diseases, including Alzheimer's. In his book about AD, Porter Shimer says, "By preserving our bodies, we are helping preserve our minds."[7]

Four areas are regularly noted by researchers as important for good health. The first is eating well. Low-fat diets that include many fruits and vegetables are recommended. They provide the vitamins that are needed for strong bodies and minds.

The second suggestion is to keep one's mind active. When talking about the brain, people often say, "Use it or lose it." If the brain is not busy, it may become diseased. Learning new things every

Activities that stimulate the mind, such as jigsaw puzzles and reading, may help prevent the onset of Alzheimer's.

day creates new brain connections. This can be done by playing an instrument, learning a new language, reading daily, or having interesting hobbies. Studies show that people who are lifelong learners have some protection against AD.

The third idea for maintaining a healthy body is regular exercise. Sports and running are good, but regular walking is encouraged. David Snowdon studied a large group of nuns to learn about AD in the aging process. He wanted to find out what they did to stay healthy throughout their lives. He discovered they all walked several hours a day. He writes, "When people ask me 'What is the first thing I should do to age successfully?' I reply, 'Walk.' Exercise protects your heart, bones, and brain."[8]

Finally, having friends and belonging to clubs and community groups supports a positive view of life. Scientists are finding that this connection with others also adds to a healthy lifestyle and may keep people safe from Alzheimer's and other diseases.

Better Diagnosis

While some researchers explore an AD vaccine, improved drugs, and the advantages of a healthy lifestyle, others want to find improved ways of diagnosing AD. They believe that if they can delay the onset of symptoms by five to ten years, they can cut the number of AD cases by as much as 75 percent. If they can find cells early on that might develop into AD, they might be able to prevent the disease. Machines are now able to do even more than CAT scans. Two newer systems are called MRI and PET. When used together, they are able to show 3-D pictures of the brain at work. This is a great help for early diagnosis. Blood tests that show early signs of weak brain cells are needed, too. There is hope that they will be created in the days to come. Successful research in this area could keep thousands of people from suffering the pro-gression of AD. Paula, a University of Virginia nurse who organizes Alzheimer drug studies, explains, "This is an exciting time. Researchers

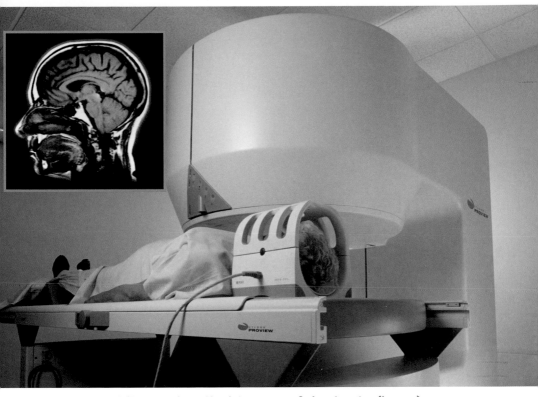

By providing a detailed image of the brain (inset), an MRI scan helps doctors detect the onset of Alzheimer's disease.

now believe that damage to brain cells may start years before symptoms appear. Scientists are now looking at ways to discover AD earlier than ever. In the future, if AD could be diagnosed before symptoms appear, new treatments could be used."[9]

The coming days will bring new facts, ideas, and discoveries to beat Alzheimer's. Success against AD is closer than ever. People who do not have AD now may never have to worry about getting it. The future is filled with hope for an end to this harmful disease.

Notes

Chapter One: What Is Alzheimer's Disease?

1. Charlie, interview with author, August 11, 2003, Takoma Park, MD.
2. Amy Hepler, interview with author, November 12, 2003, Charlottesville, VA.

Chapter Two: Diagnosing the Disease

3. Lurli Gay, interview with author, December 9, 2003, Gordonsville, VA.
4. Porter Shimer, *New Hope for People with Alzheimer's and Their Caregivers.* Roseville, CA: Prima, 2002, p. 29.

Chapter Three: Living with Alzheimer's

5. Eva Stalnacker, telephone interview with author, January 7, 2004.

6. Ben Forrest, interview with author, November 12, 2003, Charlottesville, VA.

Chapter Four: Treatment and Prevention

7. Shimer, *New Hope for People with Alzheimer's and Their Caregivers*, p. 203.
8. David Snowdon, *Aging with Grace: What the Nun Study Teaches Us About Leading Longer, Healthier, and More Meaningful Lives.* New York: Bantam, 2001, p. 38.
9. Paula Damgaard, telephone interview with author, January 13, 2004.

Glossary

cerebral hemispheres: The rounded halves of the forward and upper part of the brain (cerebrum), also known as the left brain and the right brain.

contagious: Having a disease that can be spread from person to person.

dementia: Major loss of memory and thinking skills that causes problems with daily life.

diagnose: To decide what disease a person has by means of a medical exam.

genetic: Having to do with genes, the basic units of the features passed down from parents to their children.

hippocampus: The part of the brain that transfers information into memory.

infection: Disease caused by coming in contact with harmful germs.

plaques: Sticky clusters of protein deposits and dead and dying brain cells; found in the brains of people with AD.

prevention: Stopping something from happening.

progressive: Passing from one stage to the next.

research: The study of a subject to find new facts.

Safe Return: A program of the Alzheimer's Association that provides identification bracelets for AD victims that wander.

symptoms: Signs of something; in medicine, signs of a certain illness.

tangles: Twisted pieces of protein inside brain cells, found in AD sufferers.

treatments: Medicines, therapies, surgeries, and care programs to deal with disease.

vaccine: A liquid created to prevent a disease. It is put into the body by needle; a shot.

For Further Exploration

Books

Mary Bahr, *The Memory Box.* Morton Grove, IL: Albert Whitman, 1992. Zack is spending the summer with his grandparents. He finds out that Gramps has AD. Gramps finds a way to help Zack keep memories of their good times together.

Susan Dudley Gold, *Alzheimer's Disease.* Rev. ed. Berkeley Heights, NJ: Enslow, 2000. This book tells what Alzheimer's looks like, how it affects families, and how to deal with it.

Kim Gosselin, *Allie Learns About Alzheimer's Disease: A Family Story About Love, Patience, and Acceptance.* Plainview, NY: JayJo, 2001. Allie's granny is becoming more and more forgetful. When she comes to live at Allie's house, Allie learns all about AD.

Elizabeth Weitzman, *Let's Talk About When Someone You Love Has Alzheimer's Disease.* Center City, MN: Hazelden/PowerKids, 1998. Weitzman explains the effects of AD on people and tells children what they can do to cope with the illness.

Web Sites

Alzheimer's Association (www.alz.org). This Web site of the Alzheimer's Association can answer any questions about AD. The resources in the kids and teens section are especially good.

Alzheimer's Disease Education & Referral Center (www.alzheimers.org). This Web site is provided by the National Institute on Aging. The caregiving heading will lead to AD information for children and teenagers.

Index

About the Author

Barbara Webber lives on a hilltop overlooking the Southwest Mountains in central Virginia. She shares her home with her best friend and their cat, Emmet. She was a children's librarian for more than twenty years. She also taught elementary school students for six years. When not writing, Webber enjoys gardening, reading, storytelling, and traveling.

For ten years she was caregiver for her mother, who suffered from Alzheimer's disease. Though her mother passed away in 2001, Webber maintains an interest in AD research. This is her first book.